What It Means

TO

Be Southern

A Reflective Perspective
From a Girl Raised Southern

by Cecilia Budd Grimes

What It Means
TO
Be Southern

Published by
Abram & vanWyck Publishers
North Carolina
www.EtiquetteMatters.com

Manufactured in U.S.A.

Design by Paula Chance, Atlanta, GA

Library of Congress Control Number 12288343
ISBN 0-9708396-0-X
Second Edition

WITH SPECIAL GRATITUDE to Michelle Ray, who in 1997, on my birthday no less, asked me to include a short talk, perhaps ten minutes in length, on *What It Means To Be Southern* during a staff development session at the historic Carolina Inn in Chapel Hill, North Carolina. That suggestion is one of the most significant birthday gifts I've ever received. The response to that little talk, in the years since that time, has yielded repeated requests to present the topic in an expanded form to other audiences in a wide array of venues and then to create a book version. To her I give the credit for the idea, the topic, and the title of the book. What a very special gift! Bless your heart, Michelle, and thank you.

Another debt of gratitude I owe is to Paula Chance, with whom it has been a pleasure to work. She seemed to understand intuitively what I was attempting to do, and when I discovered she grew up in Mississippi, I knew why. To her I give the credit for the look of the book and its layout and design. Thank you, Paula, for your gracious gift of a Southern collaboration.

~

Table of Contents

~

MANY THANKS to Jacquie Ebeling of the Old North State Club for sharing this quote she proudly displays on a wall in her North Carolina home:

> *"I'm not from the South,*
> *but I got here as quick as I could!"*

Our first grandchild is Alaina Budd Grimes. Her middle name is the same as her great-great-great-great grandfather's, who went on to his reward on June 26, 1891. His final resting place in Chatham County, North Carolina, is located less than 30 miles from where she was born on June 26, exactly one hundred and five years later.

~

A lady from Georgia married into our family. She came from a family in which all the daughters were named for flowers. She was Violet; her sisters were Daisy, Iris, Rose, and Nolia, short for her given name, Magnolia.

On a menu for one of my Southern programs, there was a listing for Cheddar Grits. That was a dead giveaway the creator of the menu was not from the South. If you grew up Southern, you know to call the dish "Cheese Grits" (even if the cheese you use is Cheddar, which it often is). Grits are pulverized dried corn to which cheese, milk, and butter may be added.

Mary John's Cheese Grits

~3~

1 cup of quick grits
4 cups of milk
2 cups of sharp cheese, grated
1 stick of butter
dash of Tabasco sauce

Combine grits, milk and salt in a saucepan
and boil for 3 minutes. Add the cheese,
butter, and Tabasco sauce.

Pour into a small, lightly greased
baking dish or ovenproof bowl.

Bake for one hour at 325°.

"Bless Your Heart"

AND

"Y'all Come"

*Favored Phrasing
from the Mouths of Southerners*

SOUTHERNERS are quickly identified with a couple of phrases, *"Bless Your Heart,"* appropriately decreed for a variety of situations, and *"Y'all,"* pronounced as one syllable.

"Bless your heart" is a kind and gracious response to another's fortune, good or bad. Bless your heart would be a Southerner's response to someone who had just won millions of dollars in a sweepstakes, watched a beloved dog get run over, received a job promotion, or misplaced car keys. Southerners also revert to the phrase "Bless your heart" when they don't know what else to say.

> *"My arthritis is really acting up these days."*
> *"Bless your heart."*

> *"We are so excited that Jake has been accepted at college."*
> *"Bless his heart."*

> *"Our daughter has decided to postpone her wedding."*
> *"Bless her heart."*

Southerners always search for the right words, and *"Bless your heart"* is priceless and always correct.

Y'all is the Southern contraction for "you all,"
and generally is addressed toward a group, as opposed
to a single person. Plural may be signaled more
conclusively by "*All y'all.*" As a convenient and
kind-sounding reference, y'all is also favored by
Southerners who wouldn't want to offend when names
aren't immediately known or recalled.

> *"Y'all come by the house after the game.*
> *We'll have some ham biscuits and iced tea."*

We *mash* our potatoes, and we *mash* elevator
buttons. We also *mash* light switches, or *we'll cut the
lights on* for you or *cut the lights off,* whichever is needed.
We *tote* things, as in "*Anna Kathryn was so kind to tote
my heavy groceries to the house.*" We *carry* people to the
grocery store, and we let you know what we're getting

ready to do by announcing, *"We're fixin' to . . ."* I find myself is a common comment, as in *"I find myself thinking it's Tuesday, when it's Wednesday."* We'll greet you with *"Hey"* and we'll likely add the preposition "up" to our verbs. We *call you up*, we admonish you to *listen up*, and we invite y'all to *come on up* to the house, and *"Goodness gracious"* we hope you come!

We also crack our windows, and we trim our pencils, and we like to set a spell.

In the South you just might find in one of those little country stores the most delicious pecan pie you ever tasted—right on the same shelf as the fishing bait. That's because somebody's grandparents know both things are in high demand.

Plan on eating the best green beans you ever put into your mouth down South. The secret, of course, is the fatback that's used for seasoning. Southern cooks just whack a slice of fat from their country ham, with maybe just a little meat on it, and toss it in the pot. Country hams are cured with salt and sugar, so there's no need to add anything else except a little pepper. We call that pretty fine eating. Most Southern cooks have gotten over the need to keep a tin canister by the stove to pour up their bacon grease, but they haven't gotten over needing fatback.

"Ugly
AS
Homemade Sin"

And Other Southern Ways of Putting It

IT'S PRETTY MUCH accepted that Southerners talk differently. Some even say we talk funny and I'm not sure it's the pace of our words. When we're having a conversation, we try to be specific when we we're explaining things, so we use points of reference that are easily understood. When we say we haven't seen you in a month of Sundays, no further explanation is necessary. It really has been a very, very long time.

Other Southern slang includes...

naked as a . . . jay bird

sharp as a . . . tack

thin as a . . . rail

dead as a . . . door nail

smart as a . . . whip

looks like something . . . the cat drug in

running around like a chicken . . . with its head cut off

tight as a . . . tick

Other expressions you're likely to hear from a Southerner:

"lope the roads"

That's what my mama and her sister, Barbara Anne, like to do. They get into a car and ride around, shop, and visit. It is not necessary to have an established itinerary before departing. It's a keep-on-the-move, unplanned adventure that provides worthwhile subjects for story telling later on when you're asked, *"What'd y'all do today?"*

"traipse"

When you traipse, you traipse around. One doesn't just traipse, one traipses around or traipses about. (The preposition is necessary for clarity.) Gad about is almost the same thing. A car is not necessary for traipsin' or gaddin' about; a car is necessary for lopin' the roads.

"smidgen"

An inexact amount, a smidgen is a measurement for just a bit of something. The Restoration Hardware Company recently advertised a set of measuring spoons for a pinch, a smidgen, and a dash. Most Southerners would enjoy them for sentimental reasons. They probably wouldn't actually need to use them.

"piddlin'"

Sometimes used as a verb, "just piddlin'," which is to say not doing anything of great importance, but staying busy with activity, or as an adjective as in "piddlin' amount," which is to say an amount not large enough to really count.

"Y'all Better . . ."

Growing up on South Second Avenue

Some of the Rules We're Taught to Live By

GROWING UP SOUTHERN, early on, you're taught **The Rules**. Others might think of them as traditions, but from a Southerner's perspective, they are iron-clad and not subject to much negotiation. The decrees come from Mama, Daddy, Granny, Great-Granny, the aunts, and the ladies in Mama's Better Times Bridge Club.

~14~

Be proud you're a Southerner. Acknowledge it as a downright privilege.

When I'm asked about the South, I offer this general geography lesson: North Carolina, South Carolina, Georgia, Alabama, Mississippi, Louisiana, Arkansas, Tennessee, Kentucky, and Virginia and parts of Texas, particularly the eastern side (Patrick Swayze is from Texas; he's definitely Southern); the uppermost parts of Florida, particularly around the panhandle which, after all, does border Georgia and Alabama (other parts are generally acknowledged as a retirement destination for people from all over the country); and parts of West Virginia, specifically the lower portion that tucks between Virginia and Kentucky.

If I were asked to differentiate between the various designations of the region, I'd offer these: the Old South (what used to be), the Deep South (mostly the lower Southern states, where drawls are quite pronounced, most likely Alabama, Mississippi, and Louisiana, Georgia, and probably South Carolina), Down South (a somewhat vague reference to the geography of the region, as it relates to other parts of the country) and the New South (the emerging Atlanta-based commerce center). If others from outside the region take issue with these descriptions, I'd just smile.

Always capitalize references to the South: a Southerner, the South, Southern foods, Southern ways, and *Southern Lady*, *Southern Living*, and *Southern Accents*, magazines that contribute to our way of life. Contrary to stated rules of grammar or how references to the South are spelled in newspapers or magazines originating in other parts of the country, the "S" is always written in upper case to denote its status in the hearts and souls of its children.

Show proper deference by answering "Yes, ma'am" or "No, sir" to adults. Stand when adults enter the room. Show respect to your elders; it's an important part of your upbringing. When last names seem too formal (a next-door neighbor of twenty-five years), we may use a first name by adding Miss or Mr., as an honorific, to the given name, as in *"Miss Gladys,"* or *"Mr. John."* Manners are a very big issue to Southerners. In fact, we tell our children *"Don't be ugly,"* which has nothing to do with their precious appearance, but rather reminds them that *"Pretty is as pretty does,"* a maxim repeatedly heard in the South. They're also reminded that how you behave has a direct bearing on how your people are regarded. Well-mannered children reflect their upbringing.

Pay your respects to the dearly departed in more ways than one. Pull over to the side of the road when approaching a hearse and the subsequent line of mourners following behind. In respect to the dearly departed, wait until all have passed before resuming your journey. If you know the family well, you're probably in the line of mourners yourself, and if so, you'd have already taken a dish of food, possibly deviled eggs or a Co-Cola salad, to the bereaved family.

Mark the seasons with appropriate footwear. Bring out the white shoes for Easter (which is the first Sunday after the first full moon after the first day of spring) but put them up (which is to say put them away) on Labor Day. There are notable exceptions for wearing white shoes out of season—when working out in the gym or walking down the aisle to meet the groom, for example.

Speak glowingly of others, when possible. When conversing with others, select adjectives that are appropriately kind but full of nuance. In glowing terms, "precious, lovely, and darlin' (without the 'g')" are the three adjectives you'll most often hear in flattering terms; they denote things that are praise-worthy and truly first-class. Lesser admired things may be termed "nice" or "cute," which is marginal praise at best, but sounds all right. The use of "perfectly," as in "perfectly nice," is subtle but may indicate mild displeasure. Sweet, as in "sweet tea," assumes that sugar is added to the iced tea, but sweet otherwise is not particularly complimentary. In the South, we prefer our children to be "precious" (instead of sweet), their manners to be "lovely" (instead of nice) and things in our home to be considered "darlin'" (instead of cute). A Southern lady would rather have a lovely disposition than a sweet one.

My friend at a little shop here in town has a grandson she calls "Precious." The last time I was in her shop buying ribbon, I asked her if her little grandson had given her a special name. *"Oh, sure,"* she replied. *"He always calls me Precious."*

Jennifer Kay Wells, aged two, sitting in her mama's grocery buggy in Atlanta, was approached by a friend and asked, *"Darlin', are you shopping?"*

Little Miss Jennifer replied, in true Southern style, *"No, I'm precious."*

The Paschals were hosting a Saturday morning brunch to welcome a new bride into the family. They were all known to be first-class cooks, going all the way back to Mrs. Paschal's mother, Mrs. Huddleston, whose Sunday dinners I remember from my childhood. Because I knew the hostesses, all five of them, were Southern ladies, I inquired about the number of deviled egg plates they owned collectively. Mrs. Paschal joined me shortly at the dining room table where I was raving about Matilda's light, flaky biscuits.

"It's 42," she answered, *"but we didn't count the Tupperware carriers we all have. We figured you were just interested in the really pretty ones."*

Deviled Eggs

6 large eggs
1 heaping tablespoon of sweet pickle chips
1 heaping tablespoon of mayonnaise
a pinch of sugar
a pinch of salt
1/2 teaspoon of celery seed

Boil the eggs for 14 minutes and remove
from heat. Rinse boiled eggs in cold water
to cool. Peel the shells off the eggs.

Slice the eggs in half lengthwise.
Set aside. Remove the yolks
and flake with a fork.

Add all the other ingredients and mix well.
Heap the yolk mixture into the egg white
shells. Chill before serving.

*A splash of vinegar in the water
will prevent the eggs from spewing,
something eggs often do in boiling water.

Most grocery stores in the South will stock sweet pickle chips (and bread and butter pickles), green pepper jelly, persimmons, and, of course, pimento cheese. You might have a hard time locating such things elsewhere. Pimento cheese is something Southerners really adore, and toasted pimento cheese sandwiches are the best.

In our little community, we still have the Farmers Alliance Store, located on the corner of the main street downtown and directly across the street from the Methodist Church that burned a few years back. Since 1888, the store has been in business selling clothing, gardening supplies, plants, bulbs, and grocery staples. They have two storefront doors, and the one on the right is where you enter to buy cheese. You just walk on back and look for the big wooden box that holds the wheel of cheese. They'll fix you right up. They even have jars of pimento right there on the shelf nearby.

Four generations of my family have bought cheese at the Farmers Alliance Store.

"Don't You Dare . . ."

Some of the Rules We Don't Break

DON'T YOU DARE talk about anybody in a small town. They are "liable to be kin." That's what my granddaddy used to say and he should have known. He was the town doctor for forty-four years, and he was right. My next door neighbor, Dr. Wrenn, is a half-brother to my across-the-street neighbor, who is a cousin to my mama's sister's husband. On the other side of my family, my daddy's sister's husband was a cousin to the lovely Galloway sisters. At Daddy's funeral service, Mrs. Marion Galloway Wren sat with our family, being kin and gracious and kind. She's also distant kin, by marriage, to the Wrenns in town who spell their name with 2 n's—the ones in my neighborhood who are kin to the husband of Mama's sister. (She's the one that likes to lope the roads with Mama.) The tags on the gifts from Mama's sister's family always read, "The Wrenn Kin."

Don't you dare return a dish of food empty; it's considered downright ungracious and tacky. As part of Southern hospitality, there's a lot of food sharing. If someone dear to you has "passed away" or "gone on to their reward," you can expect your friends and neighbors in the South to come pretty quickly with comfort food. Usually within hours of the start of grieving, you'll have ham biscuits, deviled eggs, at least one pecan pie, and a pound cake on your kitchen table. Napkins and paper towels are quite likely to appear, as are jugs of tea and a cooler of ice. Southerners understand that you have so much on your mind during such trying times, and preparing food is something that your friends can do for you. Southerners will cook for days on such occasions. It's not just your hearts that will be heavy-laden; your Southern neighbors and friends will see to it that your table is heavy-laden with lots of good food when the relatives and friends start coming to call.

Our funeral homes even dispense pre-printed logs to the home of the bereaved so that all the food can be recorded. If someone has been gracious enough to send food, reciprocity must prevail. The rule that a dish that contained food cannot be returned empty is relaxed at bit on grieving occasions. A thank you note in the dish counts because the bottom of the dish is technically covered, but when you write . . .

Don't you dare send a thank you note that has a big Thank You, usually in gold, blazed in a fancy font across the front cover of the card. That is considered tacky. The use of the term "tacky" is ubiquitous, which is to say it's everywhere, but that's because it's an all-inclusive term used to describe any-thing not appropriate. A person knows a thank you note by its warm expression of gratitude, not because of being forewarned on the front cover. Ideally the note card would be an informal, a white or light ecru paper, with the writer's full name embossed or engraved across the front of the folded note paper. In my garden club, which has recently celebrated its seventieth year, the members continue to be listed by their husband's names, even those who have been widows for over twenty years. That's the same way with lots of Southern ladies and their note cards, too. It's their husband's full name, preceded by the honorific Mrs., that appears on the front of their informals.

Don't you dare give your "official" wedding gift at a bridal shower. A shower gift and a wedding gift are two distinctly different items. The gifts a Southern bride truly covets are the ones she's selected herself. So for showers, we're reminded to give the bride practical things for her new home like a toaster or monogrammed towels. For a wedding gift, we are taught to select something impressive and grand, like a piece of the bride's sterling flatware, a stem of her crystal, or a selection from her "fine" china pattern. Everyday china can go either way—it's an everyday item, so it qualifies for a shower gift, but it's selected by the bride so it can also be an appropriate wedding gift, especially if it's a big item like the platter or the gravy boat.

~

There's another rule that has faded away over the past several generations. Old timers will tell you about how they were taught not to wash clothes between Old Christmas (December 25) and New Christmas (January 6). It was thought to do so invited death into the family in the coming year. Washing clothes "between the Christmases" used to be one of those "Don't You Dare" Rules, but it's rarely observed anymore.

And don't y'all dare go barefooted until after May 1!

Greens, Hoppin'-Johns, AND Pork

Eating for Health and Wealth in the New Year

ONE OF THE TRADITIONS of growing up Southern is eating properly on New Year's Day. In order to ensure good health and fine fortune, Southerners are taught to eat three specific foods on the first day of the year to ensure a year of prosperity.

*Greens** (such as collards or turnip greens) symbolize "green backs," the term for money. Eating greens ensures a year in which money is not a worry. Eat greens on the first day of the year and money comes.

Hoppin'-Johns, the term given to a dish of black-eyed peas (sometimes combined with rice or bits of green pepper and onion), symbolize coins and assure a pocketful of change. Some Southern cooks even tossed pennies into the pot when cooking the peas. (Southern cooks knew that copper pennies would not be toxic.) Eat your Hoppin'-Johns, as the saying goes, and the coins will follow.

Pork, sometimes "hog jowl" (the fleshy, hanging part under the jaw of a pig) or "sow belly" (pork from the belly of an adult female pig), is the meat of choice. Sausage counts, as most assuredly do country ham biscuits and barbecue, a staple of any Southerner's diet, New Year's Day or not.

A certain type of bread is not specified, but cornbread and biscuits would be customary.

Miss Ella, a Southern lady who cooks what we call in the South a "mean mess of greens," taught me to put a couple of whole, unshelled pecans into the water when cooking greens. The pecans absorb the odor sometimes associated with cooking collards.

The Collard Club

Our Small Town Tradition

IN OUR LITTLE SOUTHERN community, many of the gentlemen gather on New Year's Day for an official welcoming of the New Year according to Southern tradition. Most of the charter members have long ago gone to their reward, but their children are (and eventually we expect their grandchildren to be) counted among the club's membership.

Much of the goings-on at the Collard Club is highly secretive, so we women of the town know little of the details. What we do know is that membership is by invitation, and the event is a marathon day of watching football games on television while the men feast on the proper New Year's Day greens and pork.

There's also an elaborate awards ceremony centered on the presentation of collard leaves. Awards are in three tiers: a collard cluster earned by members for extraordinary service to the community or state; a collard leaf earned for special service to the

community, and the collard stem, stripped of its leaf,
for the member who has departed from club rules (or
broken the faith as they put it) during the past year.

Each collard award, accented with a bright red bow, is
ceremoniously pinned to the deserving member's
shirt.

It's all about prosperity and ushering in the
New Year in accordance with Southern tradition,
and after the holidays, the ladies welcome a day off
from cooking.

Spoon Bread, Pecan Pie,

A N D

Other Foods Favored in the South

and Shag Dancing at the Beach

VIRGINIA SPOON BREAD

2 cups of milk
1 cup of plain corn meal
1 teaspoon of salt
1 tablespoon of sugar
2 tablespoons of shortening
(half butter/half Crisco is what I use)
3 large eggs, separated
2 teaspoons of baking powder

~

Place the milk in a saucepan and cook
on high heat until a milk film begins to bubble
to the top. At that point, remove the scalded
milk from the heat and add the corn meal.
Stir until thickened. Add the salt, sugar,
shortening, and beaten egg yolks.
When thoroughly blended,
add the baking powder and then gently
fold in the stiffly beaten egg whites.

Pour into a well-greased, ovenproof bowl
and bake for 20-25 minutes at 400°.
Serve hot with a spoon.

Serves 6.

~35~

GRANDMOTHER LUTHER'S
PECAN PIE

(a recipe passed to me by a childhood friend)

1 cup of brown sugar
1/2 cup of white sugar
1/2 stick of margarine and 1/2 stick of butter,
melted together
2 eggs, slightly beaten
2 tablespoons of milk
2 teaspoons of flour
1 teaspoon of vanilla extract
1 generous cup of chopped pecans

Blend sugars and flour.
Add the eggs, milk, and vanilla. Blend well.

Add melted butter, stirring well.

Fold in pecans.
Pour into an unbaked pie shell.

Bake 35-40 minutes
(or until center is firm) at 325°.

CO-COLA SALAD

2 small boxes of cherry gelatin
1 8-oz. package of cream cheese,
softened and cut into small pieces
1 large can of Bing cherries, drained and seeded
1 large can of crushed pineapple, drained
1 cup of pecans, chopped
2 small bottles of Co-Cola

Combine the juices from the
cherries and pineapple and heat.
Dissolve the gelatin in this
warmed mixture. Let cool.

Mix the fruit, pecans, and cream cheese
together and add to the gelatin mixture.
Blend well. Pour in the soft drink colas
and mix well. Chill until firm.

DIANA'S
BARBECUE SAUCE

3 tablespoons of vegetable oil (not olive oil)
2 cloves of garlic, finely chopped
1 large onion, finely chopped
1 cup of tomato catsup
1/2 cup of red wine vinegar
1/3 cup of freshly squeezed lemon juice
1/4 cup of Worcestershire sauce
1/4 cup of brown sugar
4 teaspoons of chili powder
2 teaspoons of celery seeds

Heat oil in sauce pan
and sauté garlic and onion.
Add remaining ingredients.
Lower heat and simmer
uncovered for 15 minutes.

Store in the refrigerator.

When asked what was for dessert, a Southern lady might respond, *"Just (ches') pie."* Most Southern cooks could whip up a chess pie with little notice because all the ingredients were kept on hand.

CHESS PIE

Cream together:
1/2 cup of butter, softened
2 cups of sugar
Add 1 tablespoon of all-purpose flour (or cornmeal).
Stir until well mixed, but do not beat.

Add 4 eggs, one at a time.
Stir in 1/2 teaspoon of vanilla extract.

Pour into a double-baked pie shell, and bake at 350° for 45-50 minutes, or until set. (Add a couple of tablespoons of lemon juice for a lemon chess pie.)

The key to this pie's success is to "double-bake" the pie crust. Place the pie crust in a pie pan, cover completely with tin foil (with a bit of a collar standing up) and fill with dry beans. Bake at 400° for 4-5 minutes. Remove from the oven, save the dry beans (which can be re-used for this same purpose) and discard the tin foil. Return the crust to the oven and bake 2 more minutes, or until beginning to golden.

Nuance and the Carolinas . . .
Barbecue, Shag Dancing,
and Beach Music

Two categories of regional significance for the North Carolinian are knowledge of two distinctly different types of barbecue, one version from the eastern part of the state and one version from the western part of the state, and shag dancing, most often associated with Carolina beaches and its distinctive music.

Barbecue from the western part of the state, generally called "Lexington Barbecue," is accompanied by a vinegar-based slaw, commonly called red slaw. Barbecue from the eastern part of the state is accompanied by a mayonnaise-based slaw, commonly called white slaw. Whichever barbecue you prefer, its name is correctly spelled *barbecue*, with a "c," and properly cooked over wood, not with electricity. Its often-used abbreviation is Bar-B-Q, which probably gave rise to the alternate phonetic misspelling (barbeque) of barbecue.

Shag dancing is a beach-born phenomenon whose popularity continues to rise. In the South, it's taught at cotillions right along with the waltz and other fine dances. Shag dancing is characterized by swiftly executed twirls, dips, and tip-toe steps synchronized with a partner. Beach music is still mighty popular in Myrtle Beach, South Carolina, and especially with those who learned to shag dance while visiting Sonny's Pavilion.

A Moon Pie

AND

RC Cola

Southern Soft Drink Rituals

A MOON PIE is made with corn syrup, flour, sugar, shortening, salt and baking soda. It's a Southern sandwich of sorts, a marshmallow smashed between two large glazed cookies. We have Tennessee to thank for this Southern treat, a favorite since it was introduced by the Chattanooga Bakery around 1919. Mr. John Shelton Reed, noted Southern scholar, reports in his book, *1001 Things Everybody Should Know about the South*, that over 50 million moon pies are sold each year. On the cover of a Moon Pie, you'll see "The Only One on the Planet!" right below the logo. Most often you'll hear a moon pie mentioned with an RC Cola. They go together just like a rose and a Baby Ruth.

Where I grew up, carbonated beverages were always called soft drinks to distinguish them from hard drinks, specifically liquor or white lightning. North Carolina claims fame for two fine soft drinks, Cheerwine, which originated in Salisbury, and

Pepsi-Cola, which originated in New Bern. Coca-Cola, which came from Atlanta, was another brand name, but we always called it Co-Cola—three syllables, not four.

There is a Southern soft drink ritual that confounds lots of people from other parts of the country. We fill our soft drinks with peanuts. We just rip open a package of salted peanuts, pour them right up to the rim of the bottle, and then take a swig.

That was THE WAY to drink a Co-Cola.

If we didn't have peanuts, we could drink our soft drink with a pack of Nabs. Today I hear people ask for cheese crackers—those small cheese cracker squares with a peanut butter filling. We still ask for Nabs where I live.

NASCAR (National Association of Stock Car Automobile Racing) owes its roots to the hard liquor (moonshine or white lightning, produced in stills) that was transported over the mountains in the South in the trunks of fast moving cars. Competitive racing was a natural outgrowth of this need to move an illegal product quickly and without interruption down winding roads. Stock car racing has been called one of the fastest growing sports in the world, and Southerners acknowledge it as part of their heritage.

Your Daddy

IS

Your Best Man

Plans Complete For Budd-Grimes Vows Saturday

Plans are now complete for the July 17 marriage service of Miss Cecilia Anne Budd and John Franklin Grimes, III at eight o'clock in the First Baptist Church of Siler City. Rev. C. R. Smith Jr., pastor will perform the ceremony.

Music will be provided by Ellihu E. Sloan, Minister of Music at the church, and Mrs. Mark Ollington of Chapel Hill, soloist. Organ selections including "Chorale and Prayer" from the Suite Gothique by Boellman, "Sheep May Safely Graze" by Bach, "Traumerei" by Schumann, "Chorale in E" by Franck, and "Supplication" by Frysinger will begin thirty minutes prior to the service. Vocal numbers by Mrs. Ollinger will include "The Greatest of These is Love" by Ware, "Entreat Me Not To Leave Thee" by Gounod and "The Lord's Prayer" by Malotte.

Out-of-town guests expected for the wedding include Mr. and Mrs. Victor Alridge and Mr. and Mrs. John Lambert of Raleigh, Mr. and Mrs. Alton Yates Lennon, Mr. and Mrs. Hadley Badgett and Becki, Miss Sharon Bain and Bob Leonard, and Mr. and Mrs. Bill Tate of Winston-Salem, Miss Kay Taylor of Fayetteville, Miss Betty Lewis of Madison, Martin Richwine of Richmond, Va., Mr. and Mrs. Jack Workman of Staten Island, N. Y., Miss Juanita Williams of Spencer, Miss Sara Webb and James E. Rogers of Greenville, Carroll Haywood of Concord, Mr. and Mrs. Hollis Franks and Robert, Mr. and Mrs. George Stone, Mr. and Mrs. Charlie Bledsoe, Mr. and Mrs. Bud Gourley, Mrs. Charlie L. Carroll, Sr., Miss Linda Dance and Miss Margaret Keese, all of Greensboro, Mr. and Mrs. Albert Long, Jr., of Durham, Miss Alice McNeill of Charlotte, the Misses Mary Sue and Jo Ann Moricle of Reidsville, Dr. and Mrs. S. A. Bell and Miss Nan Bell of Hamptonville, Eugene Wilson Brown and Mr. and Mrs. Charlie Crumley of Chapel Hill, Major and Mrs. James Elliott and daughters of Washington, D. C., Miss Marcia Black of Alexandria, Va., and Dr. J. Ollie Edmunds of Deland, Fla.

The Way We Do Weddings in the South

SOME TRADITIONS quickly signal a Southern wedding from a wedding in other parts of the country. For one thing, a Southern groom almost always asks his father to be his best man at his wedding. In other parts of the country, a groom will ask his best friend or a fraternity brother or a colleague from work to stand beside him at the altar. That's pretty much unheard of in the South, as a Southern groom thinks his daddy is the best, and therefore the Best Man for the job.

Other members of the extended family have their places, too, in a Southern wedding. Cousins on both sides of the family are asked to be bridesmaids or groomsmen, and the cake knife is turned over to the aunts as soon as the bride and groom have cut the first piece, as the aunts are in charge of slicing the cake for all the guests. Other friends of the bride's family (usually ladies from the bride's mother's garden club or bridge club) pour the punch. The punch at my wedding was the same color as the bridesmaids' dresses. A mother of the bride in the South is very attentive to such details.

Many Southern weddings a few decades ago were held on Sunday afternoons a few hours after preaching on Sunday. The people from the florist would come in after everybody had left from the morning worship service and set up the flowers and altar candles. The reception would be in the fellowship hall of the church, which was usually downstairs or in a building on the grounds.

In our little Southern communities, it was not unusual for a wedding to be held during the week. I have a friend who was married on a Wednesday because the father of the groom was our town's only pharmacist and the drug store closed on Wednesday afternoons. My mama and daddy wed on a Thursday. It is only recently that Southern weddings have moved almost exclusively to the weekend.

Times have certainly changed other things, too, with people no longer as prompt about responding to an R.s.v.p., a required courtesy included in a wedding invitation so the family will know how many people to expect. When I married several decades ago, the local newspaper published many of the details prior to the wedding. People looked forward to weddings not only to celebrate a young couple's intentions, but also as an occasion to see family and friends, especially those who were "coming in" from out-of-town. The week before my July wedding, the newspaper helped them along in this endeavor by listing by name every person from out-of-town who had accepted the invitation to attend the wedding. This same article listed the musicians by name and printed the titles of the organ selections and the vocal numbers the guests could expect to hear. My daddy used to always say that there were two things that people always remember: one is who comes to your weddings, and the other is who comes to your funerals.

Emily Grace was getting married, and I was so excited. It was summertime, and I was just dying to see Emily Grace's gifts, a fact I mentioned to my grandmother. Within the hour, my Granny Thomas arranged an afternoon visit through a telephone call to Emily Grace's mother, her dear friend.

No one needed to remind me to dress up; I knew it was to be a special occasion.

Arriving at the front door, we were greeted by Emily Grace's mother, who graciously received us into the house and remarked how kind we were to want to come to see Emily Grace's lovely wedding gifts.

And into the library we were ushered, with its handsome walnut walls, twelve-foot ceilings, and impressive display of sterling silver, china, and crystal.

It took a girl's breath away! Years later, I had to call
Emily Grace in her home in Virginia to find out what
her other patterns were, because that day, the things
I most remembered were the rows and rows of sterling
silver flatware, Old Maryland Engraved by Kirk. The
iced-tea spoons, in all their glory, were strictly aligned
in a long, precise formation, flanked by the beautifully
crafted knives, forks, and spoons. Bouillon spoons, and
soup spoons, and serving forks, and on each and every
exquisite piece of sterling, there was, at the bottom of
the handle, a small rectangular area, surrounded by
scrolling petals and cascading leaves, left fresh and
blank, expressly waiting for those exquisite new initials.

Granny Thomas soon realized that I needed more
time than she to absorb all this wedding fare and its
implications for a Southern girl. She knew it was a
necessary part of my Southern upbringing, and it
should not be rushed. With an invitation from her

hostess, she and Emily Grace's mother retired to the living room for a sip of tea. Before they withdrew, however, Emily Grace's mother offered me an added treat. Downstairs in the basement were Emily Grace's shower gifts. If I would like, I could slip down the steps and look at those. There the lesson was: toaster ovens, cookbooks, and bathroom towels, even monogrammed, were not intermingled with the REAL stuff upstairs. And besides, back then, a shower gift was never a wedding gift. Shower gifts were the practical and the functional, things all young brides needed to create their nest: dish towels, and spatulas, and bath mats, and waffle irons. A truly prized wedding gift proclaimed its status; it was sterling silver, lead crystal, or fine china, glistening and gleaming on crisp, white cloths, and found upstairs in the room with draped white floor-length cloths.

As we were walking away from the house, Granny

and I had an important conversation, for it was there that I confided to my grandmother that I thought Emily Grace had the most beautiful silver pattern in the world, and that I could not imagine anything more beautiful or finer gracing a dinner table. When I got married, I declared, I wanted to have silver just like that.

To which, my dear Granny Thomas, a Staunton, Virginia, born-and-bred Southern lady replied, *"Well, that settles that. Old Maryland Engraved it shall be. And besides, it's never too soon to select your silver pattern. Sterling silver makes wonderful graduation gifts."*

Giving Directions

How to Get to the Methodist Church

SEVERAL YEARS AGO the beautiful Methodist Church located on the main street of town burned. It was an old church, dating back to the 1920's, and was noted for its exquisite stained glass windows. In response to the tragedy, the Methodists appointed committees and within a few years built a beautiful new church on the edge of town. It's been the talk of the town, everybody being so proud and all. As you might imagine, lots of people return to town and want to view the new Methodist Church.

Here's how a local might give directions to this new building:

"You are just going to love that beautiful new Methodist Church, and it's just so lovely of you to ask. They've worked real hard these last few years, and we're all around here just so pleased with it. You're going to love it, too.

"Now we're on Dogwood Avenue. Just go right on up this hill, and you'll see a large white two-story house on the

left. That's the Wrenn home where Mrs. Virginia Mae Cross lives. She was my third-grade school teacher, and she keeps the nicest yard. Her roses out the back on that slap-white picket fence are just to die for. You oughta take a glance at them on your way by. I keep wishing she'd enter the pretty red ones in the state fair. Don't you think it's just amazing how they display them in Co-Cola bottles for the judging. Turn right there.

You'll pass the Boling houses, that's Mr. Boling, Sr.'s house on the left and the Boling son and his family live in the house on the right. Except that when Mr. Boling recently retired, the house was sold to the Paschals 'cause there was some kin there, by marriage, and they wanted that lovely rock house to stay in the family. Everybody always is just so interested so I should tell you that Miss Frances Bavier, that's Aunt Bee from the Andy Griffith Show, bought that big house next door to the Boling, Sr. home. She made our little town famous when she came to live here, and you just wouldn't have believed the traffic on that street, people riding by all the time just hoping to get a glance or two of her. I mean on Halloween night they sent a special policeman over there just to help with the crowds going to her door. She remembered the police department in her will, too.

Well, go on past her house, and keep on going down the hill until you reach the stop sign, and take a left.

You're almost in sight of the new Methodist Church, but this morning I was talking to Peggy in the grocery store. She and I are in the same bridge club, and she's a Methodist and she was on one of the committees for the new church. She told me that the parking lot is scheduled to be paved this morning, and they've blocked off the entrance so the trucks can do their work. So even if you went by this morning, I don't think you'd be able to get to see the *church today. But you come back soon anyway. Those*

stained glass windows are worth the trip alone, and we'd just

love to have y'all, you hear."

A Southern heritage continues

Being Southern is more than where you're born.
It's an idea that seems imparted at birth.
It's more than loving biscuits, and favoring barbecue,
and following rules for going barefooted.
Based more than a little bit on geography, it's a gift we
inherit over the generations from our families and friends.
It is those who came before us who taught us
What It Means To Be Southern.
Bless their hearts.